JERUSALEM

PALPHOT

Contents

Acknowledgements:
We are grateful to all those who assisted in the publication of this up-to-date book:

Photographers, Publishers, The Israel Museum, Jerusalem, The Israel Department of Antiquities, The Holyland Corporation, Jerusalem, The Temple Institute Jewish Quarter, Old City Jerusalem, The Tower of David Museum, The Nature Reserves Authority and other Museums and Institutions.

© Copyright Palphot Ltd. P.O.B. 2, Herzlia, Israel.

palphot@palphot.com, www.palphot.com

Printed in Israel.

Photographers: L. Borodulin, M. Bertinetti, W. Braun, Itamar Grinberg, E. Maestro, D. Harris, Z. Mautner, Garo Nalbandian, R. Nowitz, S. Mandrea, J. Sahar, D. Tal & M. Haramati, A. Shabataev.
Drawing: E. Barashkov.

ISBN 965-280-078-3

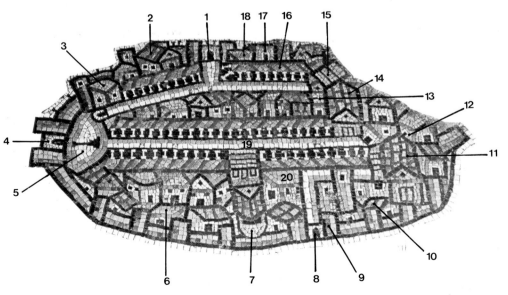

Part of the Madaba Mosaic map from the 6th century showing Jerusalem.

1 St. Stephen's Gate
2 St. Ann's Church
3 Church of St. Mary Magdalene
4 Damascus Gate
5 The Column
6 Monastery of Theodorus
7 Church of the Holy Sepulchre
8 Jaffa Gate
9 The Citadel
10 Palace of the High Priest Caiphas
11 Zion Church
12 Petros Tower
13 Dung Gate
14 Nea Church
15 Western Wall
16 Temple Mount
17 Golden Gate
18 Antonia Fortress
19 The Cardo
20 Market

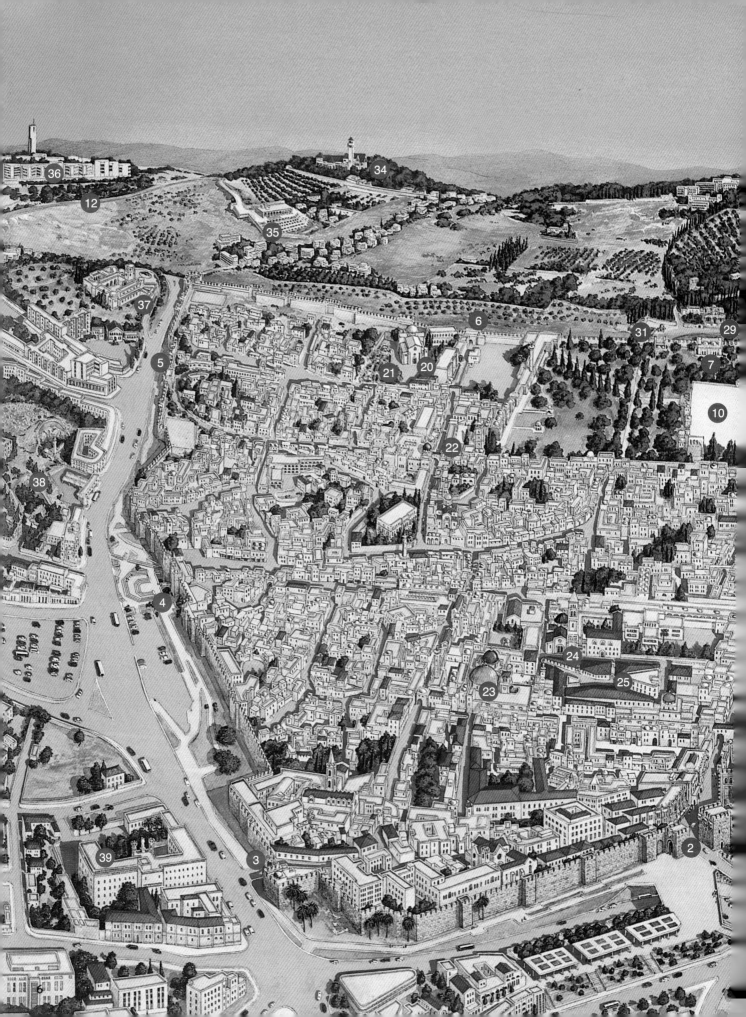

INTRODUCTION

There is a saying that "There are ten measures of beauty in the Universe, nine belong to Jerusalem, and one to the rest of the world. Whoever has not seen Jerusalem in her glory has never seen a beautiful city in his life."

Holy to Judaism, Christianity and Islam, Jerusalem, the city of one hundred names, and one thousand faces is undoubtedly the jewel in the crown that is Israel.

There is not another city that has been the cause of so many armed conflicts as Jerusalem.

King David made Jerusalem his capital. The First Temple was built there by his son Solomon during the years 961-922 B.C. It was the cultural and spiritual home of the Jewish people.

After the Babylonion conquest Jerusalem lay in ruins. The Temple was destroyed and the Jews were exiled, returning in 537 B.C. to build the Second Temple, which was completed in 517 B.C. The Temple Mount complex was enlarged and adorned over the years. It became a splendid holy site, one of the wonders of the world.

The soldiers of the Roman Tenth Legion stormed Jerusalem in 70 C.E. The city was once again in ruins, and the magnificent Second Temple was razed. Bar Kochba's revolt during 132-135 C.E. was a desperate attempt by the Jewish people to rally, but they were unable to survive the might of the Roman armies. In 135 C.E., Aelia Capitolina was built in place of Jerusalem, ruled as a Roman colony. Jerusalem was at a low ebb for the next two centuries until in 326 Emperor Constantine and his mother Helena, having converted to Christianity, came on a pilgrimage to the Holy Land, renamed the city Jerusalem and built shrines commemorating events in the life of Jesus. Under the Byzantines the city flourished but in 614 the Persians invaded the country. In 637 Jerusalem was taken over by the Moslems who built the Dome of the Rock on the site of Solomon's Temple. The Crusaders ruled the city from 1099 to 1187 when they were ousted by Saladin. His rule was followed by the Mamelukes until 15127 when Palestine became part of the Ottoman Empire. The Jews established their first settlement outside the Old City walls in 1860.

Today holy sites which are revered by the three great monotheistic faiths are a constant draw to pilgrims from all over the world.

Jews the world over pray in the direction of Jerusalem. Christians connect Jerusalem with the last year's in the life of Jesus. Here he taught, was arrested, crucified and resurrected. Moslems associate Jerusalem with El Aksa, the point from which Mohammed is believed to have ascended to the Seventh Heaven. After Mecca and Medina, Jerusalem is Islam's third holiest city. Jerusalem's sanctity and mysticism have inspired prophets, artists, poets and scholars for centuries. Nowdays it has become a major cultural centre with museums, galleries, theatres, cinemas, and also universities and yeshivot.

The presence of the supreme legislative, administrative and judicial bodies have made it into a modern capital. Sophisticated stores compete with oriental bazaars for the attention of shoppers. The variety of costumes which rub shoulders in its streets - Hassidic capotas, Moslem jalabiyas, dozens of different monks' robes, denim jeans, and many, many more - can only be matched by the

Jerusalem, by Jan Janssonius, 1657

infinite motives which move people to inhabit or visit Jerusalem. The harmony of church bells, the muezzin's call to prayers, communal study in yeshivot, and dealers offering their wares all combine in this cosmopolitan city where there is always something old or something new to be investigated. The hustle and bustle of the town, the noisy local markets, the sanctity of the holy places, and a close association with the Bible all wait to be experienced by travellers of all ages and interests from all walks of life. Each subject chosen in this book enhances the undeniable charm that belongs to Jerusalem and its environs. Traversing time, from the past to the present, the Holy City

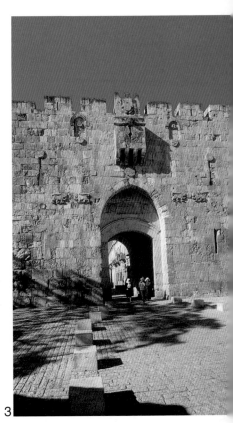

- inhabited since time immemorial - can still be called one of the most significant capital cities in the world. It is indeed an Eternal City - a gathering point for tourists, visitors and pilgrims at all times of the year.

THE GATES

There are eight gates in the Old City walls.

The Damascus Gate - which is the most ornate, is considered by many to be the most beautiful. It was built by Suleiman the Magnificent in 1537. The road to Damascus used to start here.

The New Gate - is the only gate that was not built by Suleiman. It was opened in 1889 to facilitate passage from the Christian Quarter to the Catholic institutions outside the walls.

The Jaffa Gate - this was the starting point of the road to Jaffa, an important port town, and so an outlet for trade.

The Zion Gate - connects the Armenian Quarter with Mount Zion. It has also been called the "Jewish Quarter Gate" because of its proximity to the Jewish Quarter.

The Dung Gate - this is the nearest gate to the Western Wall. It is low and narrow - just wide enough to permit the passage of a man and his donkey. Much of the city's refuse is taken to the Kidron Valley by an ancient sewer which runs beneath this gate.

The Golden Gate - is situated in the east wall of the Temple Mount enclosure. It is sometimes also called the Gate of Mercy. The gate was sealed many years ago by the Turks. Jewish tradition holds that the Messiah will enter Jerusalem through this gate.

The Lions' Gate - is named after the pair of lions who guard it. The gate is also known as St. Stephen's Gate; according to tradition he was martyred nearby.

Herod's Gate - is named for a mistaken identification of a church nearby as the home of Herod Antipas. Decorated with a roselike design, it is called in Hebrew "The Gate of the Flowers". It was closed until 1875.

1. *Jaffa Gate*
2. *The Golden Gate*
3. *Lion's Gate*
4. *Dung Gate*
5. *Herod's Gate*
6. *Zion Gate*
7. *The New Gate*
8. *Damascus Gate*
9. *Jerusalem's ramparts*

5

6

8

THE CITADEL

On the western side of the Old City the massive structure of the Citadel looms large and overpowering. It stands on the site where Herod built his palace at the end of the first century B.C. The enormous stones comprise some of Herod's most impressive and important fortifications. Only this part of the city walls remained intact after the destruction of Jerusalem by the Romans.

The Tower of Phasael, just inside the Jaffa Gate, is a Jerusalem landmark to this day. From the roof of this tower there is a wonderful view of the Old City. Flights of steps lead to the walkway which runs round the top of the Old City walls. This rampart walk has been divided into four routes; each one provides a breathtaking view of the Old City of Jerusalem.

Inside the Citadel restoration has been carried out. The refurbished halls now house the Tower of David Museum, which traces the history of Jerusalem over 3,000 years, using audio-visual programmes and modern exhibits. During the summer months a Sound and Light show entitled "A Stone in David's Tower" unfolds the dramatic story of Jerusalem in the courtyard of the museum.

Below: The Citadel during a Sound and Light Show

Views of the Citadel

The Western Wall showing the path leading to the Temple Mount and the Dome of the Rock

19

In the Western Wall tunnels

Opposite: *Prayers and festivities by the Western Wall*

ARCHAEOLOGY AND EXCAVATIONS

The southern and western wall excavations adjoining the El-Aksa Mosque have revealed many interesting features of the construction of the city. The remains of the huge Robinson Arch can clearly be seen. It is now believed that a staircase from this arch led to Herod's Basilica. These entrances were used by Herod when he entered the city. Wilson's Arch connected the Temple to the Upper City. An archaeological park has been laid out along the southern wall of the Temple. Easy paths and plaques with clear explanations make walking here an enjoyable and informative way of spending leisure time.

Opposite: *The excavated stairway leading to the Temple Mount*
Below: *The archaeological park. There are plaques with clearly marked explanations at many points along the broad paths.*

THE WESTERN WALL

The Western Wall in the Old City is all that remains of the Second Temple. Pilgrims gather from all over the world to pray at this sacred shrine. The great Herodian stones rest one on top of the other without cement between them to hold them in place. More than half of the wall is below the present day ground level.

During the years that Jerusalem was controlled by the Jordanians (from 1948-1967) access to the Wall was forbidden. After the reunification in June 1967 the site was cleared, the crowded hovels around it were pulled down, and a vast paved plaza was constructed. This has now become a meeting place for communal prayer and many public celebrations. The Western Wall is never deserted. At any hour of the day or night, winter or summer, one can always find Jews there, standing in front of the Wall in devout prayer - or placing their messages in the cracks and crevices between the stones.

THE OLD CITY

The Old City of Jerusalem is composed of four quarters, each with its own distinctive characteristics. The Christian Quarter is in the north-west; the Moslem Quarter in the north-east; the Armenian Quarter in the south-west, and the Jewish Quarter in the south-east.

These four quarters, covering an area of approximately 850 dunams, are surrounded by the city walls. Built of huge blocks of grey stone, the present walls were constructed between 1536 and 1539 during the time of Suleiman the Magnificent, the Ottoman ruler.

THE JEWISH QUARTER

Excavations in the Jewish Quarter have revealed untold treasures. Parts of the wide colonnaded street, the Cardo Maximus, have been uncovered. This was once the main thoroughfare of the Roman-Byzantine city. A mosaic map of sixth century Jerusalem was found in Jordan in 1884. This portrays the colonnaded streets and buildings of the time; it is known as the Madaba Map. A replica of part of this map (P.8.) can be seen today at the beginning of the Cardo. Byzantine and Crusader remains in the reconstructed Cardo have been incorporated into the modern structures which now stand on the original paving stones.

There is evidence of the way in which the Jews lived in Jerusalem until the destruction of the Second Temple. The Burnt House, which contains relics of one of the priestly families, is all that remains of the homes in the Upper City which were razed by the Romans in 70 C.E. Remains of Israelite walls and an Israelite tower have also been found. After the victory of Saladin in 1187, life for the Jews became easier. Synagogues and centres of learning were built - a thriving Jewish community was established, only to be destroyed once again during the Jordanian occupation of Jerusalem from 1948-1967.

Today the Jewish Quarter contains reconstructed synagogues and yeshivot - together with modern apartment buildings and houses. All are tastefully built around paved courtyards and well kept gardens - the old and the new blending together in a delightful fashion.

Above: One of the Sephardi´synagogues in the Jewish Quarter of the Old City
Below: Part of the restored Byzantine Cardo in the Jewish Quarter of the Old City.
Opposite: The Old City Wall, archaeological park, the reconstructed Jewish Quarter and the Temple Mount. In the background, the Mount of Olives

The Golden Menorah in the Cardo
The first golden seven-branched Menorah made since the destruction of the Temple, by the Temple Institute, Jerusalem (Donated by Vadim Rabinovitz)

THE TEMPLE MOUNT

For the three major monotheistic religions, the Temple Mount is the historical and spiritual focus of Jerusalem. It is revered by Jews as the holiest place on earth. The rock at the centre of the Temple Mount (now covered by the Dome of the Rock) is the place where Abraham prepared to sacrifice his son, Isaac. Solomon built the First Temple here, and later the Second Temple was erected on the same spot. Christianity associates the Temple Mount with the preaching of Jesus, whilst for Moslems this is the accepted place from which Mohammed ascended to heaven.

THE POOL OF SILWAN

Silwan, just outside the Old City walls, runs along the Ophel down to the Kidron Valley. This was the site picked by David for the establishment of his capital, Jerusalem, 5,000 years ago.

The Pool of Silwan receives water from the Spring of Gihon by way of Hezekiah's Tunnel. Since the sole source of water for Jerusalem was from this spring, it was imperative to conceal and divert the course in times of war. The second book of Chronicles 32:30 tells how "Hezekiah stopped the upper water course of Gihon, and brought it straight down to the west side of the city of David". This conduit, now known as the Silwan Tunnel, is still being used.

page 26
Above: *The reconstructed Hurva Synagogue*
Below: *The Cardo*
page 27
Silwan - the City of David
Inset: *The Archaeological Walk in section "G" of the excavations at the City of David*
Above: *The Pool of Silwan in the City of David.**
Built by King Hezekiah, this pool, quarried out of the rocks, was where Jesus sent the blind man to wash.
Below: *Hezekiah's workers cut the tunnel through the rock in order to bring the waters of the Gihon Spring inside the city walls in times of siege.*
Opposite: *The Dome of the Rock*
This magnificent mosque was built on the site of the First and Second Temples in 691 A.D. by the Omayad Khalif, Abd El Malik ibn Mirwan.
Inserts below: *Details of the Mosque*

THE DOME OF THE ROCK

One of the wonders of the world, the gold-capped Dome of the Rock is an outstanding landmark of Jerusalem. Wall mosaics, beautiful carpets and stained glass windows inside the mosque vie with the marble facade and blue and gold tiles on the outside walls of the building.

Opposite Above: *"Solomon's Stables" - part of the foundations of the Second Temple which were used by the Crusaders to house their horses.*
Opposite Below: *The interior of the El-Aqsa Mosque*

Below: *The Cupola of the Dome of the Rock. Red and gold stucco painting decorates the wood-lined cupola. A great chain hangs from the centre - all that remains of the silver candelabra that once graced the beautiful mosque.*

30

THE EL-AQSA MOSQUE

This mosque stands over an underground building called the Ancient Arcade. Built between 709-715 A.D. by Caliph Waleed, the son of Abd El Malik, the silver domed mosque is easily recognized on the southern part of the Temple Mount.

Exquisitely decorated pillars and arches support the roof; priceless rugs cover the floor. During the time of the Crusaders the mosque was used as a residence for the knights in charge of the Temple area. These knights became known as the Templars. Saladin restored the building to its original use as a mosque after the defeat of the Crusaders.

SOLOMON'S STABLES

To the east of the El-Aqsa Mosque, a flight of steps in the paved courtyard leads to the underground vaults of Solomon's Stables. The Crusaders also kept their horses here.

MARKETS

Every visitor to Jerusalem is fascinated by the bazaars and markets of the Old City. There are unlimited possibilities for bargaining. The incredible array of spices, sweetmeats, fruits and vegetables all remind the tourist that the atmosphere of the Middle East is totally different to anything that he may have encountered "at home". Stalls and stores display antiques, pottery, jewellery, carved olive wood objects, embroideries and leather work. The list is endless - there is something to suit all tastes, and all pockets.

THE VIA DOLOROSA

The Way of the Cross commemorates the path which Jesus walked bearing the cross from the Place of Judgement (Praetorium) to Calvary.

Every Friday, led by Franciscan monks, groups of Christian pilgrims from around the world retrace these steps, starting at the Church of the Flagellation and ending at the Church of the Holy Sepulchre.

There are fourteen stations along Christendom's most sacred route - each one marks an event that took place during the last walk before the Crucifixion. Nine of these points are actually along the Via Dolorosa, and five are inside the Church of the Holy Sepulchre.

Opposite: *Scenes in the markets of the Old City of Jerusalem*

Above right: *Prayers outside the Third Station of the Via Dolorosa*

Below: *The courtyard of the First Station of the Cross. Here pilgrims gather every Friday to trace the path of the Stations of the Cross*

Overleaf P. 34

Above left: *Outside the Fifth Station of the Cross where Simon of Cyrene helped Jesus carry the Cross*

Above right: *Outside the Ninth Station of the Cross, where Jesus fell for the third time. A column built into the doorway of the Coptic Church marks the site.*

Below: *The Church of the Flagellation - the Second Station of the Cross.*

Overleaf, p.35 Above right: *The Fourth Station of the Cross, The Church of Our Lady of the Spasm, where the Virgin Mary, the mother of Jesus, met Him carrying the Cross*

Above left: *The Chapel of the Second Station of the Cross*

Below right: *Part of the pavement in the courtyard of the Antonia Fortress, the remains of which are to be found in the Convent of the Sisters of Zion*

Below left: *The Stone of Basilindia. Markings on the pavement are evidence of the "King's Game" played by the Roman legionnaires.*

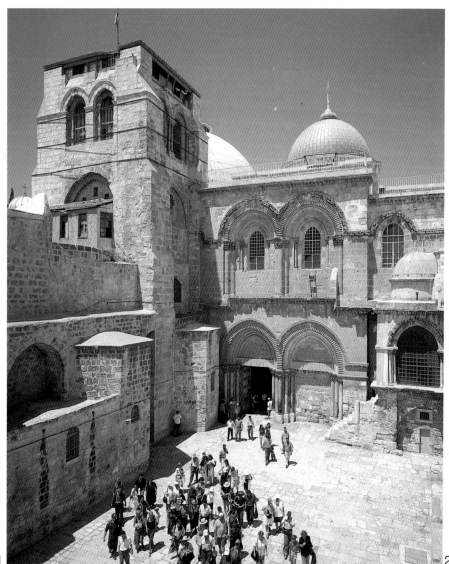

1. *The Church of the Holy Sepulchre*

2. *Interior of the Tomb of Jesus*

3. *The central dome of the Catholicon, supported by the high Crusader arches*

4. *Calvary, the Eleventh Station, where Jesus is nailed to the Cross.*

THE CHURCH OF THE HOLY SEPULCHRE

Venerated by many Christians as one of the holiest of their shrines, the Church of the Holy Sepulchre terminates the way of the Via Dolorosa. It is believed that Jesus was crucified on this spot, and here we find the tomb of Jesus.

In 325 A.D. the Emperor Constantine the Great ordered a church to be erected on this spot. His mother, the Empress Helena, discovered the tomb of Jesus after the place was revealed to her in a dream.

Three different buildings were erected - a round church, the Anastasis above the empty grave of Jesus; a basilica, the Martyrium; and the square between the two churches, a shrine marking the place of the crucifixion - Calvarium (Golgotha).

In 614 A.D. these buildings were destroyed by the Persians. They were rebuilt and destroyed once more in 1009 A.D. by Caliph Hakim. Once again they were partially restored until the Crusaders erected the present church in 1149 A.D. after their conquest of Jerusalem. Now the tomb of Jesus and the place of crucifixion are under one roof.

Below: The interior of the Church of the Holy Sepulchre

MOUNT OF OLIVES

The Mount of Olives nearby holds an important place in both Judaism and Christianity. Legend has it that the Messiah will enter the Temple Courts through the blocked Golden Gate opposite, and pious Jews have therefore chosen to be buried here to be nearby on the Day of Redemption. It was here that Jesus taught His disciples during His mission in Jerusalem - here He was made a prisoner, here He wept for Jerusalem, and here He is believed to have ascended to heaven.

The Church of All Nations close by, with its ornately decorated facade glinting in the sunlight, and the Garden of Gethsemane with its grove of ancient olive trees dating back to Byzantine times and cared for today by the Franciscan Brotherhood are important holy sites.

The village of Bethany, now known as El-Azariah, is famed as the place where Jesus performed the miracle of the raising of Lazarus four days after his death. A steep flight of steps leads to the tomb which is inside a cave. A minaret of a Moslem mosque today stands on the site of the cave.

Below: The Church of St. Anne, Bethesda. In the foreground are the excavations of the Pool of Five Colonnades - known as the Pool of Bethesda

Opposite: The Church of All Nations - Gethsemane. Amidst the trees is the Russian Orthodox Church of Mary Magdalene

THE KIDRON VALLEY

It is believed in Jewish tradition that the Messiah will come from the east, pass the Mount of Olives and continue through the Kidron Valley before arriving at the Temple Mount. All those who have died will rise on that day to escort the Messiah into the city. During the period of the First Temple, impressive burial chambers were carved into the rocks, testimony to the importance of the area. They can still be seen today.

Above: *The Kidron Valley - from the left: Absalom's Pillar, the Tomb of St. James and the Tomb of Zacharias. In the background, the Mount of Olives*
Below right: *An ancient olive tree in the Garden of Gethsemane*
Opposite:
Above left: *The Church of Dominus Flevit - "The Lord Wept". The church on the slopes of the Mount of Olives faces the Temple Mount. The present church is built on the site of the ancient church. It marks the spot where Jesus wept over the impending destruction of Jerusalem.*
Above right: *Bethany - the Church of St. Lazarus*
Below right: *The Church of the Tomb of the Virgin Mary. Built by the Crusaders, this church contains the tomb of the Virgin Mary.*
Below left: *The Chapel of the Ascension - marking the traditional spot where Jesus ascended to heaven*

THE CHURCH OF ST. PETER IN GALLICANTU

The church, built in 1931, stands on the accepted site of the House of Caiaphas, the High Priest at the time of the arrest of Jesus. Traditionally it is believed that this is the place where Peter denied his master.

At the time of the Second Temple, steps in the courtyard of the Church of St. Peter in Gallicantu connected the City of David with the Upper City (Mt. Zion). This stairway can still be seen - excavations have revealed inscriptions and weights and measures of Second Temple times, as well as a rock-cut flagellation post.

1. The Church of St. Peter in Gallicantu
2. The mosaic-adorned interior of the Church

3. An ancient flight of stairs leading up to the Church, believed to be those trodden by Jesus on his way to trial

THE GARDEN TOMB

The tranquility and beauty of the grounds of the Garden Tomb make this site a truly meaningful place of pilgrimage for the many visitors who pass through its doors on their visit to the Holy Land.

The site was discovered by a group of British Christians. Archaeological evidence of the two-roomed Herodian tomb, the huge, deep cistern, and the skull-shaped hill, as detailed in the New Testament, all led them to believe this to be the possible site of the crucifixion and the resurrection of Jesus.

The Garden Tomb Association, with headquarters in London, was founded in 1893. To this day the administration of the Garden Tomb is carried out by this evangelical foundation.

Above: *Golgotha - the hill near which the Garden Tomb is situated. Charles Gordon believed this to be Golgotha because of the resemblance of the hill to a human skull.*
Below: *The Garden Tomb - this site, north of the Damascus Gate, outside the walls of Jerusalem, is believed by many Protestants to be the place of the Crucifixion and the Resurrection of Jesus.*

MOUNT ZION

Overlooking the Sultan's Pool, Mount Zion has always been an important point of interest for visitors to Jerusalem. Some of the shrines most sacred to Christianity and Judaism are to be found here. The black-coned roof of the Dormition Abbey stands out against the Jerusalem skyline. Traditionally it is believed that the death of Mary occurred here.

Close by is the Cenacle or Coenaculum - the Hall of the Last Supper. Jesus and his followers celebrated the Passover feast here. Beneath the Cenacle is the Hall of the Washing of the Feet, a small room which leads into a fair sized hall housing the Tomb of King David. Although it is quite possible that this is not the true grave, it nevertheless became a hallowed place for pilgrims between 1948 and 1967 when the Western Wall was in Jordanian hands and could not be visited by Jews.

Opposite - above right:
A wood and ivory effigy of the Virgin Mary on her deathbed in the Crypt of the Church of the Dormition.
Opposite above left: *The Dormition Abbey by moonlight.*
Opposite below - right: *Service in the Dormition Abbey.*
Opposite below left: *The Dormition Abbey with part of the Ramparts walk.*
Right: *Notre Dame of Jerusalem Center.*
Below: *The Room of the Last Supper.*

AMMUNITION HILL

Bounded by Sderot Eshkol and Nablus Road, near Mount Scopus, Ammunition Hill is the main memorial site commemoriationg the liberation and reunification of Jerusalem, after the Six Day War.

Some of the fiercest and bloodiest fighting took place here. The Hill, in Jordanian hands from 1948-1967, was the key to East Jerusalem and the garrison on Mount Scopus. Barbed wire barriers and mined fields had to be overcome, hand to hand fighting ensued in the desperate struggle for the liberation of Jerusalem. One hundred and eighty-three Israeli soldiers fell in this battle with the Arab legion.

The Jordanian bunkers have been left as a memorial. The complex consists of an outdoor museum, public gardens and a parking lot, an underground museum, a library and an auditorium where documentary audio-visual shows in many languages are screened throughout the day.

CITY HALL

Situated between East and West Jerusalem - the magnificent complex of City Hall in Safra Square was officially opened in 1993. The work of Jack Diamond, an architect from Canada, eastern and western building styles have been skilfully combined, making use of old and new materials. The erection of two new buildings began in 1968. These were to form the main part of the new complex, whilst surrounding houses were to be restored - the ground floor being used for shops, galleries, cafes etc., and the upper stories to be converted into offices.

The whole area covers 80,000 meters. A plaza for public meetings, and for evening entertainment in the summer months has been laid out with standing space for 20,000 people, or seating arrangements for 6,000 people. Palms and brightly colored plants make a picturesque entrance to this area.

The modern offices are well equipped so that both workers and the public have every comfort. All the municipal offices are now grouped together, thus simplifying everyone's work.

Opposite
Above left: *Ammunition Hill.*

Above right - and below:
The courtyard and part of the main building of the City Hall complex.

Below left: *The Russian Orthodox Church*

Above: *The traditional tomb of King David. Pious Jews still come to pray at the tomb.*
Below: *Bird's eye view of Mt. Zion.*

Bird's eye view of the western section of Jerusalem. In the foreground, Montefiore's Windmill and Yemin Moshe. In the background, some of Jerusalem's leading hotels.

The Bronze Fountain.

Close to the delightful neighborhoods of Yemin Moshe and Mishkenot Sha'ananim there is a small square surrounded by well kept gardens. Stone benches provide seating for a pleasant half-hour of relaxation. In the centre stands one of the few fountains to be found in Jerusalem. Children love to play here throughout the year - cooling themselves in the hot summer months, and climbing on the bronze lions in the winter. The walls of the Old City, David's Tower and the Montefiore windmill provide a background that is filled with historical interest.

New housing projects are constantly springing up in West Jerusalem. Constructed from Jerusalem stone, the domed and arched buildings - the works of leading Israeli architects - blend into the landscape; the **Mamilla Project** is one such housing complex. Close to the Laromme Hotel the **Liberty Bell Garden** was laid out to mark the 20th anniversary of the independence of the U.S.A. Stone pergolas outline an open air stage where summer festivals take place. A replica of the Liberty Bell is found near the entrance to the gardens.

Opposite

Above: *David's Village - a luxury housing project. In the background, the Citadel.*

Below - right: *Yemin Moshe Quarter with the King David hotel in the background.*

Below - left: *The Liberty Bell Garden and the Inbal Hotel.*

Below: *Bronze fountain - a gift from the people of Germany erected in Yemin Moshe in 1989.*

Above right: *Yemin Moshe Quarter.*

Above: The Ramot neighbourhood
Below: Shopping in Mahane Yehuda, one of Jerusalem's oldest markets

RAMOT

Ramot, one of the new suburbs of Jerusalem is growing fast. Broad roads, multi-storied stone apartment houses and individual villas together with a thriving commercial centre, schools and excellent medical facilities help to make this a choice residential area. A new highway allows traffic to travel quickly and easily through rolling hills to Tel Aviv and beyond.

MACHANE YEHUDA MARKET

Machane Yehuda Market just off Jaffa Road is interesting and colorful to visit. Stalls are piled high with tempting fruits and vegetables - vendors vie with one another shouting the price of their wares. Towards the end of the day, especially on Friday before the Sabbath begins, there are real bargains for those who are prepared to wait until the last minute before purchasing their weekend provisions.

The atmosphere of the market has changed since it has been covered with a glass roof - the pathways are no longer a sea of mud, or dust and dirt but the goods are just as tempting, fresh and varied; it is always exciting to pay a visit to Machane Yehuda.

MEA SHEARIM

Another market with a completely different atmosphere is found in Mea Shearim - the District of One Hundred Gates - founded in 1872, and inhabited almost entirely by ultra-orthodox Jews. The fruits and vegetables are just as fresh and inviting but the people have retained the ways of an Eastern European hamlet. Dressed in the customary fashion, with a long caftan, knee-length socks and a round felt hat, replaced on high days and holidays by a fur "streimel", the great majority of men have beards and sidelocks, while the women and young girls wear long sleeved dresses with long skirts, and keep their heads covered with a kerchief if married. Visitors are asked to conform to the local atmosphere and to dress modestly. Yeshivot and synagogues abound; there are several ritual baths, a communal bakehouse, and other aids to community living. The framework of life in Mea Shearim is rigidly bound up with Jewish lore, starting early in the day with morning prayers. The year-long routine revolves largely around the observance of the Sabbath, the major festivals and minor fasts. However, with all its restrictions, life in Mea Shearim has a certain quality not found in any other district.

1

2

3

4

5

6

NEW JERUSALEM

West Jerusalem is becoming a lively area for tourists. There are excellent shops, from the large Hamashbir department store to the small single-family business giving friendly service. An abundance of tourist and travel agencies, shops specializing in gifts, souvenirs, clothes, books, jewelry and collectors items, alongside cafes and restaurants provide something for every one, with prices ranging from the lowest to the highest. In the evening the Midrahov (pedestrian mall) is bright with lights, music and entertainment.

Opposite: 1. The President's Residence. Set in spacious grounds in a quiet neighbourhood, the President's Residence is a dignified and impressive building in use since 1972. A large reception hall with stained glass windows is used for official occasions. Its walls are hung with pictures by Israel's top artists, whilst the panelled ceiling is painted in attractive colours.

2, 3, 6. The Midrahov - Ben Yehuda Street. This busy pedestrian mall in West Jerusalem is the meeting place for youngsters and old-timers, for locals and tourists. During the long, hot summer months, tables and chairs are set up outside the cafes and restaurants. Street entertainers bring a flavour of European gaiety to the capital city.

4. Zion Square

5. The Great Synagogue and Hechal Shlomo. Tourists and local worshippers flock to well-attended services *in the Great Synagogue, a modern building with magnificent stained glass windows. The entrance hall is often utilized as an additional prayer hall during festivals. The domed building is the seat of the Chief Rabbinate; it also houses an excellent library and a Museum of Judaica.*

Above - right: Talitha Kumi. In front of Jerusalem's main department store, Hamashbir Lezarchan, in King George Avenue, stands this reconstructed doorway of the 1868 Talitha Kumi school for Arab girls.

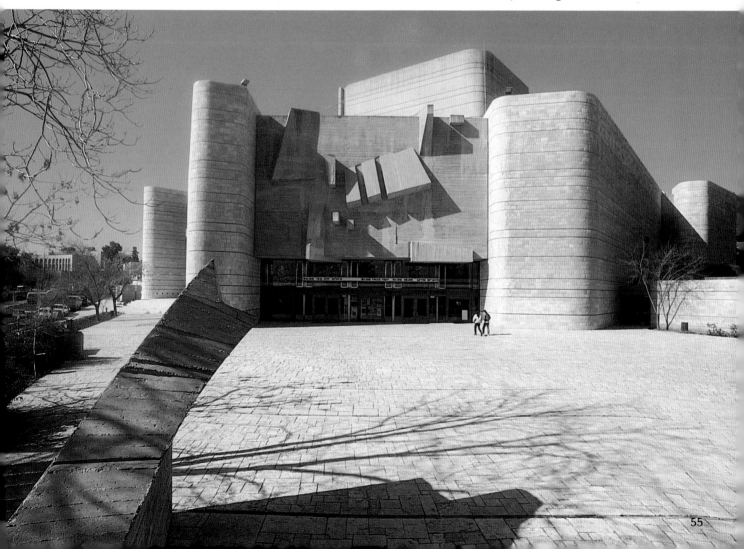

SACHER PARK

Sacher Park, a public garden near the Knesset provides wide expanses of grass, with trees for shade and paths for strolling. Families literally "move their homes" to the park for a day's outing in the fresh air. Dogs are walked, children play freely, radios and tape recorders can be heard everywhere, whilst the job for the man of the family is usually to prepare and barbecue meat for the picnic - a favourite Israeli pastime.

Opposite the park are the tall white blocks of the **Wolfson** apartment buildings. Set back from the tree-lined avenue with its constant flow of traffic, these luxury apartments with balconies overlooking the Knesset, provide spacious, elegant homes close to the commercial centre of Jerusalem.

Previous page below: The Jerusalem Sherover Theatre. Wide piazzas and striking architectural design make this theatre comparable with any the world over. The foyer is often used for exhibitions of various kinds. The theatre, the adjoining Henry Crown Concert Hall, the Rebecca Crown Auditorium and Little Theatre all have a full programme of plays, concerts and Friday afternoon films. A coffee bar and restaurant add to the theatre's facilities.

The Wolfson buildings and Sacher Park.

THE KNESSET

The seat of the Israeli Parliament, the Knesset, moved to its present location in 1966. Its sessions, three times a week, are open to the public.

The long, low building of pink Jeruslem stone was designed by Joseph Klarwein and Dov Karmi. It contains many impressive works of art. Three magnificent tapestries by Marc Chagall hang in the reception hall and he also designed the floor and wall mosaics. Facilities for the one hundred and twenty Knesset members include a synagogue, reading and conference rooms, a library and a restaurant.

The Menorah which stands opposite the Knesset was presented to the people of Israel by the British Parliament. The work of Benno Elkan, it is modelled on the seven-branched candelabrum from the Temple which the Jewish exiles carried to Rome. It depicts scenes from the history of the Jewish people and it is the official emblem of the State of Israel.

Below: The Chagall State Hall in the Knesset "Binyane Hauma" International Convention Centre

The Knesset - Israel's Parliament. Inset: the Knesset Menorah - the emblem of the State of Israel

THE ISRAEL MUSEUM

The initiative and drive of Teddy Kollek have provided Jerusalem with one of its liveliest and most functional institutions, the **Israel Museum**, which was officially opened in 1965. It is composed of four main sections - Judaica and Art; Archaeology; the Shrine of the Book and the Billy Rose Sculpture Garden.

The exhibitions, both permanent and temporary, of drawings, paintings and sculpture of modern Israeli artists are constantly being updated and enlarged, a collection of classical works is also being assembled. There is a full programme of lectures, concert and films.

The youth wing is always filled with crowds of youngsters all eager to learn and participate in the activities offered by this vibrant part of the museum. Amongst the much admired permanent exhibits is the seventeenth century Italian synagogue. During the time of the Renaissance in Italy, small but wealthy Jewish congregations erected beautiful synagogues. The furnishings and decorations were of the most elaborate workmanship and design. The fittings of the exquisite seventeenth century Vittorio Veneto Italian Synagogue have been transferred to Jerusalem, reconstructed, they are now housed in the Israel Museum - a gift from Mr. Jakob Michael of New York.

THE SHRINE OF THE BOOK

Perhaps the most important part of the Museum is the Shrine of the Book, which contains the priceless biblical manuscripts found in 1947 in caves at Qumran on the shores of the Dead Sea. Sponsored by the Gottesman Foundation, a special building was erected to house the precious scrolls. The domed, white exterior resembles the lid of one of the earthenware jars in which the scrolls were hidden; this contrasts starkly with the wall of black basalt nearby. The shrine itself is subterranean, reminiscent of the caves in which the scrolls were found.

The Bar Kochba letters, various relics and household effects found at the site of the discovery, are displayed in niches in the long tunnel-like entrance of the Shrine of the Book.

THE BIBLE LANDS MUSEUM

Dr. Eli Borowski and his wife Batya founded Jerusalem's newest museum, which was built on land donated by the State of Israel. Officially opened in May 1992 the Bible Lands Museum houses a superb collection of artifacts from ancient times. The civilizations of the Bible are shown in chronological order from 6,000 B.C.E. to 600 C.E. Each exhibit is accompanied by an appropriate Biblical quotation.

The museum logo symbolizes Genesis - the separation of the waters, and the creation of the earth, the heavens and the sea. The star represents the heavens, the dividing line represents the earth, and the waves represent the sea.

Perhaps the most exciting aspect of this modern Museum is its approach to the general public. An example is the Multimedia Seal Program, which enables the "man of the street" to understand something of the wealth of information to be gleaned from the vast collection of ancient seals contained in the museum. Computers and a comprehensive database system explain how communications developed from seals to written language to hieroglyphics to Hebrew. Modern techniques bring to life an ancient subject. New exhibitions are constantly being prepared for viewing alongside the permanent exhibits.

Above: The 17th Century Vittorio Veneto Italian Synagogue reconstructed in the Israel Museum.
Below: Finds from the Bar Kochba revolt. Jewelry box and mirror found in the Cave of Letters.
Opposite:
Above - left: Interior of the Shrine of the Book.
Above - right: The Shrine of the Book at the Israel Museum.
Below: The Israel Museum at night.

THE HEBREW UNIVERSITY

The Hebrew University, founded in 1918, was inaugurated in the presence of Lord Balfour in April 1925. The campus on Mt. Scopus included the Jewish National Library as well as faculties for the sciences, medicine, law, literature and architecture. The Hadassah hospital and nursing school were built nearby in 1939. Humming with all the activity of a lively campus, the entire complex was suddenly evacuated in April 1948 after the ambush and murder of a convoy of seventy-eight staff members of the university and the hospital.

Moving to West Jerusalem to the newly established **Givat Ram Campus**, the university continued to thrive and expand.

The new campus was officially dedicated in 1954. Modern faculty buildings are surrounded by lawns and fountains; the unusual white-domed synagogue is an outstanding landmark. Most of the students are Israeli, although each year the influx of foreign students grows stronger. **The Hebrew University** - After the Six Day War the original Mt. Scopus campus was modernized and refurnished. It has now been amalgamated with the Givat Ram Campus forming one dynamic student body - the Hebrew University of Jerusalem.

THE SUPREME COURT

Close to the Bank of Israel, within sight of the Holiday Inn Crowne Plaza Hotel (formerly the Jerusalem Hilton) the new Supreme Court stands out in stark contrast.

Officially opened on November 10th 1992, the Supreme Court has become a major tourist attraction. The building is a gift from the Rothschild Foundation. The brother and sister architectural team, Ada and Ram Karmi, were finally selected after competing against many firms in an international competition in 1986. They incorporated all kinds of architectural elements, resulting in the very specific Israeli and Jerusalem style of this building.

Above - left: *Bible Lands Museum.*
Centre - left: *The Hebrew University, Givat Ram.*
Below - left: *The Hebrew University, Mount Scopus.*
Panoramic view of Menachem Begin Highway at night.

Above: The Supreme Court.
Below: The Monastery of the Cross, with western Jerusalem
in the background

YAD VASHEM

Near Mt. Herzl, on the Mount of Remembrance is the site of Yad Vashem, the monument to six million European Jews who were murdered by the Nazis during the Second World War. On August 19th, 1953 the Knesset passed the Martyrs' and Heroes Remembrance Law –Yad Vashem, under which the Yad Vashem Remembrance Authority was set up in Jerusalem. The Authority's functions include the commemoration of the Holocaust victims, their communities, organizations and institutions, and the study and publication of the history of the Holocaust and Resistance.

The Hall of Remembrance, the Pillar of Heroism, the Synagogue, and a separate building to house the archives, the library and the administrative offices were the first to be erected. Later additions to the complex include the Hall of Names, the Children's Memorial Garden, the Avenue of the Righteous Gentiles and the Valley of the Communities.

Inscribed on the sombre grey mosaic floor of the Hall of Remembrance are the names of the 22 largest concentration camps and death camps. Beneath the Eternal Light a vault contains ashes of some of the Martyrs. Commemorative ceremonies are held here almost daily. Personalities from all over the world visiting Yad Vashem are officially received here. The Hall of Names, the Museum and the Synagogue are close by. "The Memorial Wall" by Naftali Bezem is an expression of the Holocaust of the Jewish people, its struggle and its revival in an independent state.

A memorial pillar, simple and severe in form, rises above the Mount of Remembrance, seventy feet high; it can be clearly seen from the distance. Inscriptions recalling deeds of valor are carved into the stones bordering the path leading to the pillar.

One of the responsibilities with which Yad Vashem has been charged by law is the perpetuation in Israel of the memory of the Jews who died during the Holocaust, or who fell in the Resistance. The registration of the names of the Martyrs and Heroes have been recorded by surviving relatives or friends on Pages of Testimony, which are filed in the Hall of Names. Visitors to Yad Vashem may fill such pages. In the Valley of the Communities the great blocks of stone engraved with the names of these destroyed communities pay silent homage to the millions who perished, whilst the quiet dignity of the Avenue of the Righteous Gentiles perpetuates the names of non-Jews who were imperilled trying to save their Jewish neighbours.

Above - left: *Entrance to the "Valley of the Communities",*
Yad Vashem.
Below - left: *The "Ohel Yizkor" Memorial Hall - Yad*
Vashem.

1. Yad Vashem, Statue depicting educator Janusz Korczak accompanying his young charges to their death

2. Yad Vashem, Memorial to the Freedom Fighters of the Warsaw Ghetto

3. Yad Vashem, The Children's Memorial, commemorating the one and a half million lost children

4. Tomb of Yitzhak Rabin

5. A section of the military cemetery on Mount Herzl

6. Tomb of Theodor Herzl

THE CHAGALL WINDOWS

In 1962 the French Jewish artist Marc Chagall presented to the synagogue of the Hadassah Hebrew University Medical Centre in Ein Karem a set of magnificent stained glass windows. They represent the sons of the Patriarch Jacob from whom the twelve tribes of Israel were later descended. Each tribe has its own symbols - these are portrayed in magnificent colours on the twelve panels. We are told in Genesis 49 that Jacob blessed his sons before his death. Most of the subjects in the windows derive from that story.

THE MODEL OF JERUSALEM AT THE TIME OF THE SECOND TEMPLE

The model, which stands in the grounds of the Holyland Hotel, was built before the reunification of the city. The 1:50 scale model was constructed according to the measurements given in Middot in the Mishnah, and also to fit the descriptions in the histories of Josephus Flavius. The work, using Jerusalem stone, was supervised by Prof. Michael Avi-Yonah. Changes are made in the model when excavations reveal new information. The grandeur of the city can be judged to some extent by this fascinating replica. Every detail is there, the Temple, Herod's Palace, the twin-spired Palace of the Hasmoneans, the markets, inns and common dwelling places. It is interesting to compare the Old City of today with Herodian Jerusalem.

Opposite: *Stained glass windows by Marc Chagall.*
Below: *The Model of Jerusalem at the time of the Second Temple - sited in the grounds of the Holyland Hotel.*

THE JERUSALEM MALL

The largest shopping mall in Israel, the Canion Yerushalayim in Malha, is an example of the rapid expansion in commerce and trading that has taken place during the last few years. A microcosmos of 180 shops can be found here. Fashion shops, gift shops, a supermarket, toy shops, book shops and household goods are all under one roof. For entertainment and relaxation, eight cinemas, fast food stands, restaurants and cafes complete the scene. The modern complex is spacious and well-planned - air conditioned during the hot summer months, pleasantly warm in the winter, it is a showplace of interest for all tourists, and a convenient shopping centre for local inhabitants. The Teddy Stadium closeby, together with the Tennis Centre are both welcome additions to this rapidly developing residential area in south west Jerusalem.

THE TISCH FAMILY ZOOLOGICAL GARDENS

This modern zoo near the Canion Yerushalayim in south west Jerusalem was opened in 1992 with generous

Above - left: *The Jerusalem Mall, Malha (Canion Yerushalayim).*
Below: *General view of the shopping and entertainment centre - Malha. In the background - the 'Teddy' Football stadium*

Above: *The Tisch Family Zoological Gardens. The zoo was opened in 1992 with investments from the Jerusalem Foundation, the Municipality and the Jerusalem Development Authority.*

donations from the Tisch family, and investments of the Jerusalem Foundation, the Jerusalem Municipality and the Jerusalem Development Authority. The zoo is set in spacious surroundings amidst the hills of Jerusalem. Broad paths, well marked, lead to the various exhibits. The animals are kept in open spaces in natural surroundings - low fences, or large glass windows cut into the side walls separate them from the public so there is no feeling of confinement.

An ornamental pond, surrounded by grassy terraced slopes, is the home of numerous different species of waterfowl. They rest amidst the plants growing in and around the pond. Monkeys inhabit an island close by - a waterfall cascades throughout the day.

A specially darkened hall houses reptiles and small animals. Birds fly freely in enormous aviaries.

For the children a special "petting zoo" has been established, next to a creative play centre, suitable for most age groups. Rest areas and water fountains abound within the grounds of the zoo - whilst a snack bar, a restaurant and a gift shop are all near the entrance.

THE SHEROVER AND HAAS PROMENADE (TAYELET).

A broad promenade, planned by Shlomo Aaronson, provides spectacular views of Jerusalem. Situated between East Talpiot and Talpiot, the Mount of Olives and the City of David are spread out like a vast carpet before the spectator - whilst in the background modern Jerusalem is seen. A popular meeting place, the landscaped gardens, walkways and a childrens' playground are enjoyed by all. Those who prefer to sit and admire the panorama relax in the cafe or the restaurant - in the shade of the trellised roof.

Above and below: *Views of the Tayelet. The promenade along the desert affords spectacular views of Jerusalem.*

Below right: The Church of the Visitation - Ein Karem.
Above: The Village of Ein Karem.

EIN KAREM

The little village of Ein Karem is about 7 kilometres south-west of Jerusalem. Minarets, spires and winding paths make this one of the most picturesque of spots. Known as the "city of Judah" the village is associated with the life of John the Baptist. Here Zacharias, his father, had his summer home, and here the Virgin Mary visited her cousin Elisabeth. The Church of the Visitation was built on the spot where the house was situated. The present Church of the Visitation was built in 1935 by the architect Barluzzi on the remains of former churches, the first of which was built in the fourth century A.D. and later destroyed. The forecourt is lined with ceramic tiles bearing the Magnificat in many languages.

BETHLEHEM

Bethlehem is first mentioned in the Bible in Genesis 35:19 - "so Rachel died and she was buried on the way to Ephrath" (that is Bethlehem). The town is situated about 6 km south of Jerusalem in neatly terraced countryside. The fields east of Bethlehem where shepherds graze their flocks today are accepted as those where Ruth and Boaz met in the fields of Bethlehem. Their union produced Jesse, father of David, who was born in Bethlehem. Later he was anointed as King of Israel by the Prophet Samuel.

One of the holiest sites in Christianity is the manger in Bethlehem where Mary gave birth to Jesus. Helena, mother of Constantine, the Byzantine emperor, built a church in 385 over the site of the manger. Fragments of the mosaic floor of this edifice can still be seen today.

The Emperor Justinian erected the building as it stands today. The mosaics on the wall, the wax paintings on the columns and the decorations date back to the Crusader period.

Since that time the church has fallen into disrepair. The doorway was lowered by partly sealing the Crusader arch sometime during the seventh century to ensure that Moslems could not enter the church on horseback. The visitor of today must bend almost double in order to gain access to the church.

Most Christian buildings were destroyed during the Persian invasion of the seventh century A.D., but the Church of the Nativity was saved from desecration - possibly because of the mosaic on the facade of the church which depicts the Magi in Persian dress.

RACHEL'S TOMB

Just outside Bethlehem, this is the accepted place where Rachel, Jacob's favourite wife, was buried after she died in childbirth "on the road...to Bethlehem." She is the only Biblical matriarch not buried in the family tomb in Hebron. Over the years the Tomb of Rachel has become a pilgrimage place for the Jewish people, especially barren women.

Opposite
Above - left: *Rachel's Tomb - on the way to Bethlehem.*
Below: *Shepherds' Field. To this day shepherds take their flocks to graze in the fields around Bethlehem. The pastoral landscape has changed little since biblical times.*
Above right: *The Church of the Nativity*
Center right: *Interior of the Basilica of the Nativity*
Below right: *The silver star in the Grotto of the Nativity*
Below left: *Facade of the Milk Grotto Church*

Overleaf Page 72: *General view of Bethlehem.*